舞妓 ふく乃

京めぐり
十五景

Maiko Fukuno 15 scenic spots around Kyoto

Kyoto Flower Tourism

京都フラワーツーリズム
「ふく乃会」

はじめに

日本人形のような容貌と、よく通る現代的な声。舞妓ふく乃さんの
最初の印象はその２つだけだった。日を追うごとに彼女の撮影データ
は蓄積されていく。美しく整った横顔、微笑むとペコリと凹むエクボ、
アーモンドのように形のよい瞳。撮るたびに新鮮な表情を見せて
くれるふく乃さん。洛北の木々の煌めき、渉成園の水面のブルーに
吸い込まれて消えてしまうような、儚げでピュアなふく乃さん。
撮影のあいまに楽しいことを思い浮かべ、嬉々とする愛らしい
ふく乃さん……この本は、いろんなふく乃さんを、８人で、何か月も
追いかけた記録です。

Introduction

The features of a Japanese doll and a clear contemporary voice. That was my
first impression of Maiko Fukuno. Her photos accumulate as the days go by.
Her beautiful profile, smiling dimpled cheeks, almond-shaped eyes. Fukuno
shows a fresh look every time I take her picture. Like the glistening of the
trees, sucked into the blue surface of the water at Shoseien gardens and
disappearing, Fukuno is ephemeral and pure. Adorable Fukuno happily
remembers fun times during shooting.

This book is a record of various sides of Fukuno, taken by eight people, over
several months.

睦月 むつき
January

国の登録有形文化財　堀野記念館

1月 睦月 January

1月 睦月 January

「舞：宇治茶」
舞手ぬぐいを纏う特徴的な舞の「宇治茶」
個人的に一番好きな舞。
上紅をさし、より美しくなってから舞っていただきたかったため、一年間待ち続けました。
そんな想いが詰まったふく乃さんの宇治茶です。
（gaap）

"Dance: Uji tea"
A characteristic dance "Uji tea" using a Tenugui hand towel
My favourite dance, personally.
I waited a whole year in order to see this dance after she coloured her upper lip with crimson and became even more beautiful.
This is Fukuno's "Uji tea", full of those thoughts and feelings.
(Gaap)

二、如月 きさらぎ
February

国指定の登録有形文化財　同志社女子大学ジェームズ館

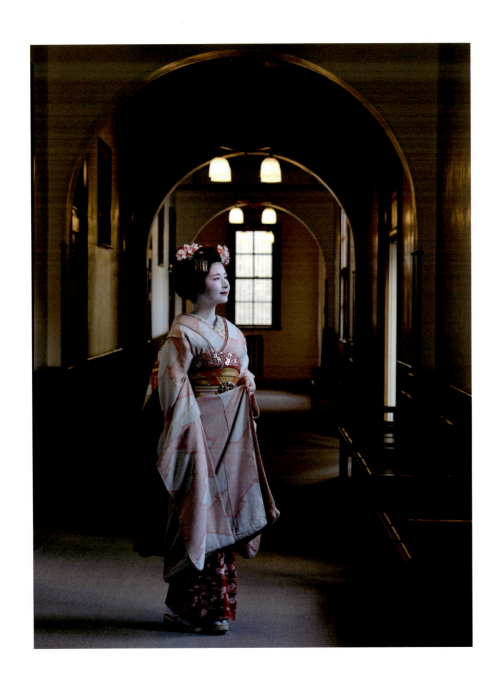

2月 如月 February

2月 如月 February 13

「同志社女子大学　ジェームズ館」

館外では落着いた煉瓦壁を背景に、薄桃色の絞り衣装と梅の花簪との対比で 愛らしく弾ける若さを強調、館内では洋館特有の光と陰の空間にたたずむ 乙女のたおやかさを表現、和風版フェルメールの世界を意図しました。

洋館特有の光と陰の空間に、アカデミズムの重厚さとは対照的な、薄桃色をまとった可愛い迷い人が現れた。その微笑がとてもまぶしくて まるで和風版フェルメールの世界だ。

（青木千春）

"Doshisha Women's University James Hall"
Outside the hall, I emphasized her youth, bursting with charm, by contrasting her to the light pink garments and plum blossom hair ornaments, against the backdrop of a low-key brick wall. Inside the hall, I expressed her maiden-like grace as she stands still within the unique atmosphere of light and shadow in the Western-style building; I intended to create a Japanese style version of Vermeer's world.

(Chiharu Aoki)

三 弥生
やよい
March

国の登録有形文化財 「冨田屋」
宮川町 お茶屋 花傳、宮川町界隈

3月 弥生 March

3月 弥生 March

「西陣そして、宮川町」
この月は幸運にも2度、ふく乃さんを撮影する機会に恵まれた。1度目は上旬、西陣の老舗 冨田屋さんにて、お座敷のひな飾りを背景に。2度目は春の訪れ、京おどりも間近な花街 宮川町でのスナップ。

(鬼界 順)

"Nishijin, then Miyagawa-cho"
I was fortunate enough to have the opportunity to shoot Fukuno twice this month. The first time was at the beginning of the month, at Nishijin's long-established store Tomitaya, with the zashiki room and doll decorations in the background. The second time was in spring, a snap at Miyagawa-cho Kagai with the Kyo-Odori Dance close at hand.

(Jun Kikai)

四、卯月
うづき
April

名勝 渉成園（枳殻邸）

4月 卯月 April

4月 卯月 April

「桜の渉成園」

天候に恵まれた4月中旬、桜の淡いピンク、木々のうす緑で彩られた渉成園を背景に「ふく乃さん」の優しい表情を引き出す写真になればと思い撮影させて頂きました。

(小森 芳行)

"Cherry blossoms at Shoseien Gardens"
A fine day in the middle of April, I aimed to take a photo that draws out Fukuno's gentle expression, with Shoseien Garden, decorated with delicate pink cherry blossoms and pale green trees, in the background.

(Yoshiyuki Komori)

五、皐月
さつき
May

重要文化財　旧三井家下鴨別邸

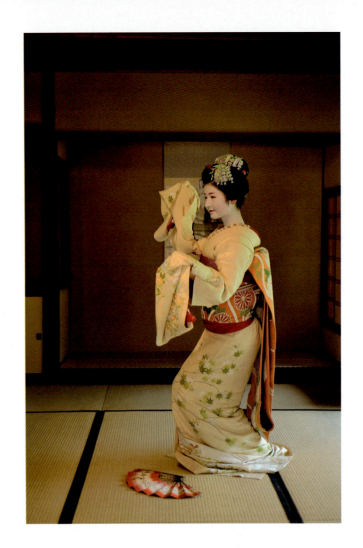

5月 皐月 May

5月 皐月 May

「旧三井家下鴨別邸」
大正時代に建てられた由緒ある建物。舞妓さんがタイムスリップした様なold風に仕上げてみました。

(石原 孝)

"Old Mitsui Family Shimogamo Villa"
A venerable building built in the Taisho era (1911-26). I tried to create an old-fashioned vibe, as if the Maiko had travelled back in time.

(Takashi Ishihara)

六 水無月 みなづき
June

名勝 渉成園（枳殻邸） 臨池亭

6月 水無月 June

6月 水無月 June

「渉成園 臨池亭」
　生来の気品ある端正な面影は、明るい藤色の裾引きと鮮やかな柳の花簪と相まって
眩しいほどの瑞々しさを四方に放つ。初夏の日差しのもと若緑を映す水辺の縁台で、
そっと彼方を見つめ恥じらいを扇で隠す横顔は一幅の画を思わせる。

(青木 千春)

"Rinchitei Teahouse at Shoseien Gardens"
Her inherently elegant and neat façade coupled with the bright wisteria hemming and brilliant willow hair ornaments brings out her youth and liveliness in full force in a way that is almost dazzling. Her profile as she gazes into the distance and hides her shyness with a fan under the rays of the early summer sun by the waterside reflecting the young green leaves is very picturesque.

(Chiharu Aoki)

七、文月（上）
ふみづき
July

立本寺

7月 文月 July

7月 文月 July

O how much more doth beauty beauteous seem, By that sweet ornament which truth doth give!The rose looks fair, but fairer we it deem For that sweet odour which doth in it live.

The canker-blooms have full as deep a dye As the perfumed tincture of the roses,Hang on such thorns and play as wantonly When summer's breath their masked buds discloses:

But, for their virtue only is their show, They live unwoo'd and unrespected fade,Die to themselves. Sweet roses do not so; Of their sweet deaths are sweetest odours made:

And so of you, beauteous and lovely youth, When that shall fade, my verse distills your truth.(William Shakespeare, 1564-1616, Sonnet 54)

(Tatas Brotosudarmo)

七、文月（下）ふみづき July

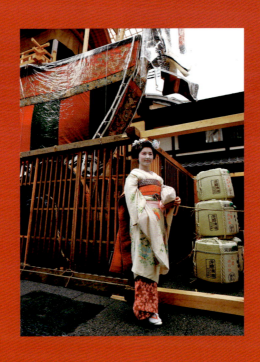

大船鉾　祇園祭

7月 文月 July

「祇園祭 大船鉾」
祇園祭、大船鉾の会所での撮影機会、祇園祭らしさと思い挑むもなかなか思うような絵、作れませんでしたが、早朝で且つ、蒸し暑い厳しい状況にも関わらず、優しい笑顔の「ふく乃さん」に救われた撮影となりました。

(小森芳行)

"Gion festival Ofune Hoko float"
I relished this opportunity to take photos of the Gion festival with the famous Ofune Hoko float, but couldn't create the work I hoped for despite my efforts. In the end, my shooting was saved by Fukuno who kept smiling kindly, despite the early start and harsh hot and humid conditions.

(Yoshiyuki Komori)

八葉月(上) August
はづき

投扇興と京町家「大西常」

8月 葉月 August

「投扇興」

江戸後期頃から流行したといわれる室内遊戯の投扇興。

ふく乃さんが投げる姿はタイムスリップしたかのような不思議な感覚でした。

(gaap)

"Fan-throwing contest"
Tousenkyo, the fan-throwing contest, is said that have been a popular indoor game since the late Edo period. It was a strange feeling watching Fukuno throw fans, as though she had travelled back in time.

(Gaap)

八、葉月(下)
はづき
August

木屋町　佛沙羅館

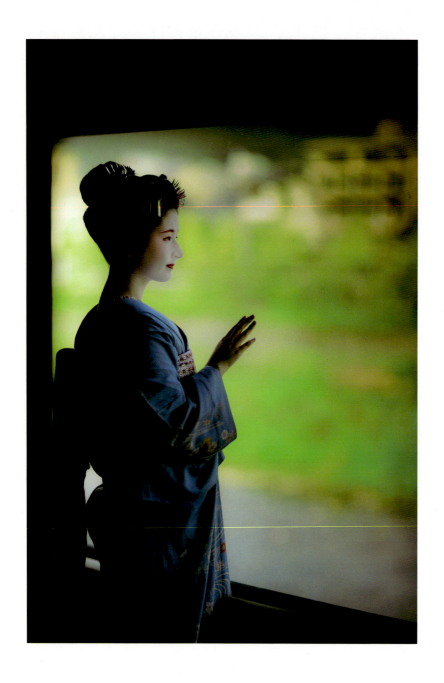

8月 葉月 August

「木屋町 仏沙羅館」
ふく乃さんと言えば「笑顔」と誰もが認めるほど
人の心を癒し　元気を与えてくれる「ふく乃スマイル」の持ち主であります
そんな彼女が夏休みも終わりの頃
学生たちで賑わう鴨川の畔を見つめる　初めて見たふく乃さんの表情を撮影させて　頂きました
　　　　　　　　　　　　　　　　　　　　　　　　　　　　　　（Mait)

"Kiyamachi Bussarakan Restaurant"
When it comes to Fukuno, you can't fail to recognize her "Fukuno Smile" that heals your heart and lifts your spirits. I shot her for the first time as she gazes at the bank of Kamogawa river crowded with students at the end of the summer vacation
　　　　　　　　　　　　　　　　　　　　　　　　　　　　　　（Mait)

九、長月 なが つき September

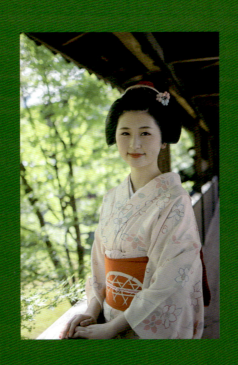

京都府指定有形文化財　本山　妙覚寺

9月 長月 September

9月 長月 September

「からげ姿」
白粉を落とした舞妓さんの素顔。
屋外では十代の少女の煌めきと青葉楓の瑞々しさを
屋内では清らかな乙女の表情を
引きずりとは違う自然体のふく乃さんを写しました。
（gaap）

"Everyday appearance"
The bare face of a Maiko without her white makeup.

Outside, I captured a relaxed side of Fukuno showing the sparkle of a teenage girl among fresh green maple leaves, different to her pure maiden-like expression drawn out indoors.
(Gaap)

十、神無月
かんなづき
October

宮川町 お茶屋 花傳、宮川町界隈

10月 神無月 October

10月 神無月 October

「宮川町・お茶屋 花傳」
まるで「お人形さん」みたい
と言う表現がぴったりの 可愛らしさと清楚さを
持つふく乃さん
そんな彼女も もうすぐお姉さん舞妓
ちょっと大人っぽい妖艶なお姿を 撮影させて頂
きました
　　　　　　　　　　　　　　　　　　(Mait)

"Miyagawa-cho Teahouse Kaden"
Fukuno, with cuteness and neatness that fits the phrase
"like a doll" perfectly, will soon become a senior
Maiko. I took a photo of her slightly mature and
bewitching figure.
　　　　　　　　　　　　　　　　　　(Mait)

十一、霜月 (上) November
しもつき

建仁寺の塔頭 西来院

11月 霜月 November

11月 霜月 November

「紅葉の西来院」
この年は紅葉の鮮やかさが今ひとつだと感じたため、紅葉や舞妓さんの全体を写すことにとらわれず、色々とアングルを変えながらベストな角度を探しました。お寺ということもあり、最初はふく乃さんの表情が堅いように思われましたが、室内から戸外へ出ると表情がやわらいだので、その瞬間を切り取りました。

(土井 啓州)

"Autumn leaves at Seiraiin Temple"
As I felt this year's autumn leaves were lacking in vividness, I decided to try various angles and the look for the best shot without restricting myself to capture all of the autumn leaves or Maiko. We were shooting in a temple and it seemed that Fukuno's facial expressions were a bit wooden at the start, but when we left to head outdoors her expressions softened, so I captured that moment.

(Hirokuni Doi)

十一、霜月（下）
しもつき
November

高台寺ライトアップ

11月 霜月 November

「紅葉の高台寺ライトアップ」

紅葉の夜間ライトアップで人気の高台寺。鏡の様な臥龍池に映り込む紅葉。
この素晴らしい場面に舞妓さんを撮りこむ機会に恵まれました。
夜間11時頃の難しい撮影でした。1枚でもいい写真が撮れる様に頑張ってみました。

(石原 孝)

"Autumn leaves illumination at Kodaiji Temple"
The popular evening autumn leaves illumination spot, Kodaiji Temple. Autumn leaves reflected on the mirror-like Garyochi Pond. I was blessed with the opportunity to take photos of Maiko at this wonderful location. It was a difficult shooting at around 11 o'clock in the evening. I tried my hardest to take be able to take even one good picture.

(Takashi Ishihara)

十二、師走
しわす
December

紫織庵

12月 師走 Decenmber

「旧川崎家 紫織庵」

大正期の和洋折衷の居住空間。2階チーク の間にて撮影。柔らかいレースの光が舞妓さん を天使のように優しくつつみこむ。

(鬼界 順)

"Shiorian Museum"
An eclectic Japanese-Western style living space from the Taisho era. Shot in the teak chamber on the second floor. Soft lace-like light gently envelops the Maiko like an angel.

(Jun Kikai)

12月 師走 Decenmber

ふく乃賞コレクション
Fukuno Award Collection

ふく乃賞（舞妓賞）は撮影会の参加者が提供するオープンデータをもとに、モデルとなった舞妓さん自身が選ぶ「お気に入り写真」に贈られる賞です。

The Fukuno Award (Maiko Award) is an award given to the "favourite photograph" selected by the Maiko model herself, based on open data provided by the photo session participants.

ふく乃さんのコメント

January ／ 1月
photo by Takashi.I

「全体のバランスが良かったです！」

"The overall balance was excellent!"

ふく乃さんのコメント

February ／2月
photo by gaap

「廊下の奥行きが出ていて素敵です。窓からの自然な
ひかりが当たっているのもいいなと思いました」

"The depth of the corridor comes out and is great. I thought that the natural
light coming in from the window is also good."

March ／3月
photo by gaap

「華やかで、楽しそうな雰囲気がいいなと思いました」

"I think the gorgeous, fun atmosphere is good"

April ／4月
photo by Yoshiyuki.K

「桜のピンク・若葉の緑、青空をイメージさせる水色の着物が写真いっぱい
に収められていて春らしい暖かくて柔らかい雰囲気がお気に入りです」

"The light blue kimono that makes you think of pink cherry blossoms, fresh green leaves, and a
blue sky appears in lots of pictures, and I like the spring-like, warm and soft atmosphere."

May ／5月
photo by Takashi.I

「いつもと少し違った感じの雰囲気がよかったです」

"The slightly different from usual atmosphere was good"

89

ふく乃さんのコメント

June ／ 6月

photo by gaap

「お庭の緑色の背景と、だらりの帯の緑色が重なって、自然に溶け込んでいるところが素敵どす。また、障子のガラスがちょうど屏風のようになっているのも可愛く思えました」

"The overlap and natural blending of the green background of the garden and the green colour of the loose sash into each other is wonderful. Also, I thought that the glass of the sliding door appearing just like a folding screen was lovely"

July ／ 7月（1）

photo by gaap

「ガラス越しに撮っていただいた写真は初めてのような気がします。きれいに写してくれはっておおきに」

"I think this was the first time I had my photograph taken through glass. Thank you for taking it so beautifully"

July ／ 7月（2）

photo by Yoshiyuki.K

「外から差し込んだ光が幻想的な雰囲気を出していていいなと思いました。この日の撮影は朝早いにもかかわらずたくさんの方に来ていただけて、とても嬉しおした。楽しい時間をおおきに」

"I thought that the light shining from the outside created a fantastic atmosphere. Regardless of the early start, lots of people came to the shoot on this day and I was very pleased. Thank you for an enjoyable time."

August ／ 8月（1）

photo by gaap

「投扇興ならではの躍動感あふれる写真が素敵です！」

"This photograph full of dynamism unique to the Tousenkyo fan throwing game is wonderful!"

ふく乃さんのコメント

August ／ 8月 (2)
photo by Mait

「ひかりの当たり具合がきれいやなと思いました」

"I thought that the light exposure was beautiful."

Septembar ／ 9月
photo by gaap

「木漏れ日がきれいでした。全体のバランスが素敵です」

"The sunlight filtering through the trees was beautiful. The overall balance is wonderful"

October ／ 10月
photo by Mait

「影が浮かび上がっておもしろいです」

"The clearly defined shadows are interesting"

November ／ 11月
photo by Hirokuni.D

「自然な感じの笑顔を撮ってくれはったので!」

"Because you captured a natural-looking smile!"

91

撮影者プロフィール

gaap
2015年12月、天候に恵まれ汗ばむ陽気で行われた事始め。
置屋「河よ志」の前で女将さんから沿道のカメラマンに出たての舞妓はんを紹介。
それがふく乃さんとの初めての出会い。
初めて見た時から変わらぬ透明感はそのままに、少女から大人へと変わりゆく姿を一枚一枚心を込めてシャッターを切らせて頂いています。

青木千春
Chiharu Aoki
天領倉敷四百年の伝統が生んだ傑作 " ふく乃さん " の魅力を写したい、その想いを素直に表現しました。無邪気な幼子のような笑顔、希望に夢見る乙女の瞳、ひたすら思い詰めるような知的な憂い顔、我が子を見守る優しい母親の眼差し。僅かな表情変化で幅広い世代を表現する " ふく乃さん " は強い存在感があります。花街の色に染まる前に、倉敷町衆文化の " 美の結晶 " を残しておきたいと念じました。

小森芳行
Yoshiyuki Komori
自動車好きが切っ掛けで写真撮影を始め、鈴鹿サーキットをホームにモータースポーツ撮影主体、その他、飛行機、花、モデルポートレート等、機材性能頼り、自己流、自己満足で節操なく何でも撮影していましたが数年前、某カメラ会社の撮影会で舞妓さんを始めて撮影。その魅力に惹かれ、年に1、2回の芸舞妓撮影会を楽しんでいましたところ、昨年はじめて「ふく乃さん」に出会い、自分の撮影技術が上達したかのように勘違いさせてもらう素敵な表情、笑顔、立ち振る舞いから、今では大半の撮影が「ふく乃さん」となりました。これからもその成長、撮り続けていきたいと‥‥‥‥。

石原 孝
Takashi Ishihara
時代の流れは速く、伝統ある京の花街においても現代の舞妓さんは何処と無く昔風ではなく明るい現代っ子的な舞妓さんです。私は毎週の様に京の花街に撮影に通っていましたが あるときに宮川町置屋『河よ志』で仕込みさんをしていたふく乃さんに出会いました。16歳にしては何処と無く落ち着いて古風な感じが非常に魅力的で興味を惹かれました。将来舞妓さんになった時にはぜひ撮影したいと思っていた折に『花なび』での撮影会の事を知り参加しました。舞妓さんになったふく乃さんは私の想像どうりの古風で魅力的な舞妓さんになっていました。 これからも芸妓さんになるまでのふく乃さんをカメラに写し記録していきたいと思っています。

Mait
千年のみやこ「京都」その伝統文化を育み守り続けてきた人々や風土
春をいろどる櫻と舞い 夏を清める鴨川の床 秋深まって移り行くもみじそして春をじっと待つ雪の白
歴史的建造物に於いて 継続的に芸舞妓さんを撮影させて頂く事で この町でくらす方々の心を 作品にしたいと思いました

土井啓州
Kunihiro Doi
岡山県津山市生まれ。カメラを最初に手にしたのは高校時代。
最初は父の影響もあり、風景を中心に撮影し、日本風景写真協会に入会。
その後、全日本写真連盟に入会し、人物写真に興味を持ち、その連盟主催による芸舞妓撮影会に参加したのがきっかけで、その美に魅了され機会あるごとに撮影会に参加するようになりました。今後は彼女達の持つ外面の美とともに内に秘めた、京都、ひいては日本の伝統文化を守ろうとする内面の力強さと美を表現出来る写真撮影を目指しています。

Tatas Brotosudarmo
Portrait of Maiko Fukuno for July 2018 by Tatas Brotosudarmo
The selection of these portraits was based on the Sonnet 54 of Shakespeare by using monochrome format that enhances beauty, elegant, tenderness, and respect combined with the cheerfulness of summer when the sun is shining with its warm. I hope that these selections of photos can depict the inner beauty of Maiko Fukuno..

鬼界 順
June Kikai
「ふく乃さんの成長を応援し撮り続ける撮影会（ふく乃会）」の発起人、ナビゲーター。

撮影地リスト

1月 キンシ正宗 堀野記念館
京都府京都市中京区堺町通二条上ル亀屋町172
TEL075-223-2072

2月 同志社女子大学 ジェームズ館
京都府京都市上京区今出川通寺町西入ル
TEL075-251-4111

3月 西陣 暮らしの美術館 冨田屋
京都府京都市上京区大宮通一条上ル
TEL075-432-6701

4月・6月 東本願寺 渉成園（枳殻邸）
京都府京都市下京区下珠数屋町通間之町東入ル東玉水町
TEL075-371-9210

5月 旧三井家下鴨別邸
京都府京都市左京区下鴨宮河町58番地2
TEL075-366-4321

7月（上）本山 立本寺
京都府京都市上京区七本松通仁和寺街道上ル1番地107
TEL075-461-6516

7月（下）祇園祭 大船鉾
公益財団法人 四条町大船鉾保存会
京都府京都市下京区新町通四条下ル四条町359番地1
TEL075-361-8130

It began in December 2015 on a fine day, just warm enough to bring out a slight sweat. The house-mother introduced a fresh-faced Maiko to a cameraman along the road in front of the okiya "Kawayoshi". That was my first encounter with Fukuno. I put my heart into each photo I take of her form as she transforms from a girl to an adult, with a sense freshness and purity unchanged from the first time I saw her.	1月「舞：宇治茶」 7月「投扇興」 9月「からげ姿」
I want to capture the charm of the masterpiece "Fukuno" born from 400 years of Kurashiki tradition. I express this feeling honestly in my works. A smile like an innocent infant, the eyes of a maiden dreaming in hope, an intellectual melancholy face deep in thought, the gaze of a mother watching over her child. "Fukuno" has a strong presence, able to represent a wide range of generations with a just a slight change in expression. I want to preserve this "beautiful crystal" created by Kurashiki town culture, before she becomes dyed in the unique colours of the 'Kagai' world.	2月「同志社女子大学　ジェームズ館」 6月「渉成園 臨池亭」
As a car lover that started off in motor sport photography, I made Suzuka Circuit my home, then moved on to other subjects, such as airplanes, flowers, model portraits etc. I was shooting whatever without integrity, relying on high-level equipment, doing things in my own way, for my own satisfaction until a few years ago when, during a photography meeting of a certain camera company, I shot a Maiko for the first time and was attracted by her charm. From that time, I enjoyed attending Maiko photography sessions once or twice a year, and then for the first time last year I encountered "Fukuno". Her wonderful expressions, smiles and manner gave me the illusion that my shooting skills had suddenly improved there and then. Now, most of my shoots are just of "Fukuno". I want to keep following and taking photos of her progress from now on…	4月「桜の渉成園」 7月「祇園祭 大船鉾」
Times are changing rapidly, even in traditional Kyoto 'Kagai'. Contemporary Maiko are no longer old-fashioned, but rather bright modern young women. I was visiting 'Kagai' in Kyoto to take photos on almost a weekly basis, but one day, I encountered a young Fukuno still in training at the okiya "Kawayoshi" in Miyagawa-cho (one of the 'kagai'). For a 16 year-old she was somehow relaxed and calm, and I was drawn to her classical charm. I definitely wanted to take her picture when she became a Maiko in the future, so when I heard about the "Flower Navi" photo sessions I decided to participate. As I expected, Fukuno had become an old-school and charming Maiko. I'd like to keep recording Fukuno's growth through my photos from now on until she becomes a Geiko.	5月「旧三井家下鴨別邸」 11月「紅葉の高台寺ライトアップ」
The people and environment that have shaped and protected the traditional culture of Kyoto, the capital for over a thousand years. Cherry blossoms and dances that colour Spring. Kamogawa decks that soothe the Summer heat. Maple leaves that deepen in colour through Autumn. White snow that silently waits for Spring. I would like to make works showing the spirit of these townspeople by continuing to photograph Geisha and Maiko in historically significant buildings.	8月「木屋町　佛沙羅館」 10月「宮川町・お茶屋 花傳」
Born in Tsuyama city, Okayama prefecture. I first got a camera during my high school years. At first, partly due to the influence of my father, I took pictures of scenery and joined the Japan Landscape Photo Association. After that, I joined the All Japan Photographic Federation, became interested in portraits, and participated in the Maiko photography session organized by the Federation. I was fascinated by the Maiko's beauty and started to participate in the photography sessions whenever I had a chance. In the future, I aim to take photos that express the Maikos' hidden inner strength and beauty that will preserve the traditional culture of Kyoto, along with their external beauty.	11月「紅葉の西来院」
Portrait of Maiko Fukuno for July 2018 by Tatas Brotosudarmo The selection of these portraits was based on the Sonnet 54 of Shakespeare by using monochrome format that enhances beauty, elegant, tenderness, and respect combined with the cheerfulness of summer when the sun is shining with its warm. I hope that these selections of photos can depict the inner beauty of Maiko Fukuno..	7月「立本寺」
	3月「西陣そして、宮川町」 12月「旧川崎家 紫織庵」

3月(上)　大西常商店
　　　　　京都府京都市下京区松原通高倉西入ル本燈籠町23
　　　　　TEL075-351-1156

3月(下)　佛沙羅館　（ぶっさらかん）
　　　　　京都府京都市下京区木屋町通松原上ル美濃屋町173-1
　　　　　TEL075-361-4535

9月　　　妙覚寺
　　　　　京都府京都市上京区上御霊前通小川東入ル清蔵口町135
　　　　　TEL075-441-2802

10月　　　宮川町　お茶屋 花傳

11月(上)　西来院
　　　　　京都府京都市東山区大和大路四条下ル小松町584
　　　　　（建仁寺境内塔頭）
　　　　　TEL075-561-5785

11月(下)　高台寺(ライトアップ)
　　　　　京都府京都市東山区高台寺下河原町526
　　　　　TEL075-561-9966

12月　　　紫織庵
　　　　　京都府京都市中京区新町通六角上ル
　　　　　TEL075-241-0215

おわりに

彼女ほど洋館の似合う女性も珍しい。

　均整のとれた美しい顔立ちがそうさせるのか、彼女のバックグラウンド、倉敷の血統がそうさせるのか、見慣れた舞妓の和服姿からは想像もつかないくらいだ。初めて洋館で撮影したときは、あまりのマッチングの良さに驚いた。そこで、私はふく乃さんに何度も洋館に足を運んでもらった。
　もともと西洋建築が好きで、仕事でもプライベートでも国内に残る"レトロ建築"を巡っていた。だから、ふく乃さんが洋館にマッチすることがうれしく、フラワーツーリズムの撮影会では5ヶ所も、京都に残る洋館等をロケ地として選んでいる（この写真集では2ヶ所を掲載）。
　一年中、観光客でにぎわう京都という土地柄、そしてガイドブック制作の経験上、「京都」の「ホンモノ」を「旬」の季節に合わせて設定する、というリクエストがいかに難しいものかを私は知っている。その点、いつもわがままを実現してくれる、プロデューサーの高木治夫氏には心から感謝したい。
　そして、「ふく乃さんの成長を応援し撮り続ける撮影会（ふく乃会）」と写真集『舞妓 ふく乃〜京めぐり十五景〜』の出版に際し、重要文化財や名勝など、唯一無二の素晴らしきロケーションを提供してくださった関係者の皆さまに深く御礼を申し上げます。

　和服が好きで京都の文化に関心があった少女は、花街という一種独特の世界に住み、大人の階段を駆け上がっていく。彼女が初めて見た舞台で感銘を受けた芸妓「ふく紘」さんのように、しなやかで強い芸妓さんになる日まで…日々お稽古を積み重ね、変化していく彼女を追いかけようと思う。

写真家　鬼界　順

鬼界　順（きかいじゅん）

京都府在住。16年間、地元京都を中心とした旅行ガイドブックの取材・執筆・撮影業務を担当。
イタリアへの撮影旅行をかさね、国内外のギャラリーやレストラン、カフェなど多様なスペースでの個展を開催。
講師として参加した撮影会にて、舞妓 ふく乃さんと出逢う。
その愛らしく、美しい姿に魅せられ「ふく乃会」のナビゲーターに就任する。
著書に『Sicilia』、『Mistero』、『舞妓と町家』などがある。
京都市芸術文化協会会員。

In closing

It is rare to find a Maiko who fits Western-style buildings so well.

It is almost impossible to imagine from the familiar kimono-clad appearance of a Maiko, but something about her beautiful balanced facial expressions, her background, or her Kurashiki pedigree just works. When I shot at Western-style buildings for the first time, I was surprised by this strong affinity. Since then, I had Fukuno visit Western-style buildings time and time again.

I originally liked western architecture, and enjoyed touring around "retro architecture" remaining in Japan both for work and on my own time. So, I'm happy that Fukuno matches Western-style buildings, and I have chosen five western-style buildings etc. remaining in Kyoto as a locations for the Flower Tourism photography events (two locations are shown in this photo collection)…

In the city of Kyoto that is coloured by crowds with tourists throughout the year, and from my experience of guide book production, I know how difficult it is to respond to the request of an "authentic", "seasonal" experience in "Kyoto". In that respect, I would like to thank the producer Takagi Haruo for realizing my selfish requests all the time.

Also, in publishing the photo collection "Maiko Fukuno - 15 scenic spots around Kyoto" and photo collection "Fukuno Club" to support the growth of Fukuno, I would like to express my deepest gratitude to all those concerned who provided important cultural properties, scenic spots etc. as unique and wonderful locations.

A girl who liked kimono and was interested in the culture of Kyoto now lives in a peculiar world called 'Kagai', and is running up the stairs to adulthood. Until the day she becomes a elegant and strong Geiko (the name for Geisha in Kyoto) like "Fukuhiro", who left a deep impression on Fukuno when she saw a traditional Geiko performance for the first time ... I will keep following Fukuno as she works hard in everyday practice and goes on to blossom.

Photographer Jun Kikai

Jun Kikai

I live in Kyoto prefecture. In charge of reporting, writing and photography for travel guide books, mainly in my home town of Kyoto, for 16 years. I take photography trips to Italy, and hold solo exhibitions in various spaces such as galleries, restaurants and cafés in and outside of the country. I first met Maiko Fukuno at a photo session where I participated as a lecturer. I was fascinated by her adorable and beautiful appearance and have taken on the role of Navigator of the "Fukuno Club". I am a member of the Kyoto City Art and Culture Association.

写 真/青木千春 石原孝 鬼界順 小森芳行 土井啓州	Photos / Chiharu Aoki, Takashi Ishihara, Jun Kikai, Yoshiyuki Komori,
gaap Tatas Brotosudarmo Mait	Hirokuni Doi, gaap, Tatas Brotosudarmo, Mait

写　　　真/青木千春　石原孝　鬼界順　小森芳行　土井啓州
　　　　　gaap　Tatas Brotosudarmo　Mait
英文翻訳/ Helena Matthews
撮影協力/キンシ正宗 堀野記念館
　　　　　同志社女子大学　ジェームズ館
　　　　　西陣　暮らしの美術館　冨田屋
　　　　　東本願寺　渉成園
　　　　　旧三井家下鴨別邸
　　　　　公益財団法人 四条町大船鉾保存会
　　　　　大西常商店
　　　　　佛沙羅館
　　　　　妙覚寺
　　　　　高台寺
　　　　　紫織庵
　　　　　宮川町　お茶屋 花傳
　　　　　　　　　　　　（順不同、敬称略）

Photos / Chiharu Aoki, Takashi Ishihara, Jun Kikai, Yoshiyuki Komori,
　　　　Hirokuni Doi, gaap, Tatas Brotosudarmo, Mait
English translation / Helena Matthews
Cooperation with photography /
　　　Kinshi Masamune Horino Memorial Hall
　　　Doshisha Women's University James Hall
　　　Nishijin Tondaya
　　　Higashi Honganji Temple Shoseien Gardens
　　　Old Mitsui Family Shimogamo Villa
　　　Public Interest Incorporated Foundation: Shijo-cho Ofune
　　　Hoko Preservation Association
　　　Onishitsune
　　　Bussarakan Restaurant
　　　Myokakuji Temple
　　　Kodaiji Temple
　　　Shiorian Museum
　　　Miyagawa-cho Teahouse Kaden
　　　　　　　(In no particular order, honorific titles omitted)

企　画　京都フラワーツーリズム合同会社
編　集　鬼界 順
発行人　高木治夫
発行日　2018年4月3日

Planning:　Kyoto Flower Tourism Limited Company
Editor:　　Jun Kikai
Publisher: Haruo Takagi
Date of Publication: April 3, 2018

Maiko Fukuno 15 scenic spots around Kyoto
舞妓 ふく乃　京めぐり 十五景

発　　行/ iBooks アイブックス　印　　刷/ iColor アイカラー
〒394-0081 長野県岡谷市長地権現町2丁目8-6
FreeDial 0120-28-2624

Copyright ©2018 Kyoto Flower Tourism All rights reserved.　無断転載を禁ず　ISBN978-4-905092-44-5　Printed in Japan

京都フラワーツーリズム『花なび』　http://flowertourism.net/